C000152372

The Twelve
of Christmas

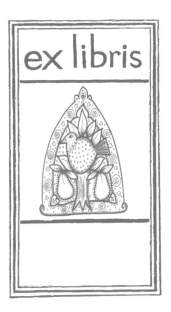

ex libris

Candlestick Press

Published by:
Candlestick Press,
21, Devonshire Avenue, Beeston,
Nottingham NG9 1BS, UK
www.candlestickpress.co.uk

Typeset and printed by Parker and Collinson Ltd.
www.parkerandcollinson.co.uk

Introduction © Carol Ann Duffy, 2009

Cover illustration 'A Partridge in a Pear Tree' from 'The Twelve Days of Christmas' © Lizzie Adcock, www.arumliliedesigns.co.uk

ISBN 978 0 9558944 8 0

Acknowledgements:
Carol Ann Duffy would like to thank Vivien Hamilton for research and Barry and Tricia Wood and Geraldine Clarkson for their generous enthusiasm.
Thanks are due to R.V. Bailey for U.A. Fanthorpe, 'Christmas in Envelopes' from *Collected Poems 1978-2003*, Peterloo Poets, 2005; Pauline Stainer for 'Carol' from *The Wound-Dresser's Dream*, Bloodaxe Books, 1996; David Higham Associates for Langston Hughes, 'Carol of the Brown King' from *Collected Poems of Langston Hughes*, Alfred A Knopf Inc/Vintage; Ohio University Press for Norman Williams, 'A Christmas Song' from *One Unblinking Eye*, Ohio University Press/ Swallow Press, 2003; The Literary Trustees of Walter de la Mare and the Society of Authors as their representative, for Walter de la Mare, 'Mistletoe'; Carol Ann Duffy and Pan Macmillan for 'December' from *Rapture*, Picador, 2005; Billy Collins and Pan Macmillan for 'Christmas Sparrow' from *Nine Horses*, Picador, 2003; Bloodaxe Books for Anne Stevenson, 'Carol of the Birds' from *Poems 1995-2005*, Bloodaxe Books, 2005 and for Denise Levertov, 'In California During the Gulf War' from *A Door in the Hive* and *Evening Train*, Bloodaxe Books, 1993. 'little tree' is reprinted from *Complete Poems 1904-1962* by E. E. Cummings, edited by George J. Firmage, by permission of W.W. Norton & Company. Copyright © 1991 by the Trustees for the E.E. Cummings Trust and George James Firmage.

The publisher acknowledges special thanks, and raises a festive glass, to Carol Ann Duffy.

Where poets are no longer living, their dates are given.

Introduction

At Christmas, many of the carols that we sing are, in fact, poems; Christina Rossetti's beautiful 'In the Bleak Midwinter', for example, or the nursery-rhyme joy of 'The Twelve Days of Christmas', each line gifting its own vivid picture into the mind - a partridge in a pear tree or five gold rings. In December, our streets seem alive with sung language. Poets - by their very calling, great celebrators - have always written Christmas poetry, regardless of faith or its absence. The Russian Nobel Laureate, Joseph Brodsky, wrote an annual Christmas poem, as did the late, much-loved U.A. Fanthorpe, whose 'Christmas in Envelopes' opens the selection here. Some poets, like Denise Levertov, find an unbearable irony between the Christmas message of peace and love to all men and the horror of War. Her 'In California During the Gulf War' remains bleakly relevant.

A huge admirer of the pamphlet-cards of Candlestick Press - in my view the most original way of delivering poetry since Poems on the Underground - I volunteered to select twelve poems for Christmas. So here is the best, most poetic solution there could possibly be to card-and-present buying at Christmas - and as a little stocking filler, I couldn't resist including this very naughty couplet by Hilaire Belloc:

May all my enemies go to hell.
Noel, Noel, Noel, Noel.

Merry Christmas!

Carol Ann Duffy
Poet Laureate

Christmas in Envelopes

Monks are at it again, quaffing, carousing;
And stage-coaches, cantering straight out of
Merrie England,
In a flurry of whips and fetlocks, sacks and Santas.

Raphael has been roped in, and Botticelli;
Experts predict a vintage year for Virgins.

From the theologically challenged, Richmond Bridge,
Giverny, a lugger by moonlight, doves. Ours

Costs less than these in money, more in time;
Like them, is hopelessly irrelevant,
But brings, like them, the essential message

love

U. A. Fanthorpe (1929 -2009)

Carol of the Brown King

Of the three Wise Men
Who came to the King,
One was a brown man,
So they sing.

Of the three Wise Men
Who followed the Star,
One was a brown king
From afar.

They brought fine gifts
Of spices and gold
In jeweled boxes
of beauty untold.

Unto His humble
Manger they came
And bowed their heads
In Jesus' name.

Three Wise Men,
One dark like me -
Part of His
Nativity.

Langston Hughes (1902 - 1967)

A Bell

Had I the power
To cast a bell that should from some grand tower,
At the first Christmas hour,
Outring,
And fling
A jubilant message wide,
The forgēd metals should be thus allied:-
No iron Pride,
But soft Humility, and rich-veined Hope
Cleft from a sunny slope;
And there should be
White Charity,
And silvery Love, that knows not Doubt nor Fear,
To make the peal more clear;
And then to firmly fix the fine alloy,
There should be Joy!

Clinton Scollard (1860 - 1932)

Christmas

What, do they suppose that everything has been said
that *can* be said about any one Christmas thing?

About beef, for instance?
About plum-pudding?
About mince-pie?
About holly?
About ivy?
About rosemary?
About mistletoe?
About Christmas Eve?
About hunt-the-slipper?
About hot cockles?
About blind-man's-buff?
About shoeing-the-wild-mare?
About thread-the-needle?
About he-can-do-little-that-can't-do-this?
About puss-in-the-corner?
About snap-dragon?
About forfeits?
About Miss Smith?
About the bell-man?
About the waits?
About chilblains?
About carols?
About the fire?
About the block on it?
About school-boys?
About their mothers?
About Christmas-boxes?
About turkeys?
About Hogmany?
About goose-pie?

About mumming?
About saluting the apple-trees?
About brawn?
About plum-porridge?
About hobby-horse?
About hoppings?
About wakes?
About 'feed-the-dove'?
About hackins?
About Yule-dough?
About going-a-gooding?
About loaf-stealing?
About Julklaps? (who has exhausted that subject,
we should like to know?)
About wad-shooting?
About elder-wine?
About pantomime?
About cards?
About New-Year's Day?
About gifts?
About wassail?
About Twelfth-cake?
About king and queen?
About characters?
About eating too much?
About aldermen?
About the doctor?
About all being in the wrong?
About charity?
About all being in the right?
About faith, hope, and endeavour?
About the greatest plum-pudding for the greatest number?

Leigh Hunt (1784 - 1859)

Christmas Sparrow

The first thing I heard this morning
was a rapid flapping sound, soft, insistent -

wings against glass as it turned out
downstairs when I saw the small bird
rioting in the frame of a high window,
trying to hurl itself through
the enigma of glass into the spacious light.

Then a noise in the throat of the cat
who was hunkered on the rug
told me how the bird had gotten inside,
carried in the cold night
through the flap of a basement door,
and later released from the soft grip of teeth.

On a chair, I trapped its pulsations
in a shirt and got it to the door,
so weightless it seemed
to have vanished into the nest of cloth.

But outside, when I uncupped my hands,
it burst into its element,
dipping over the dormant garden
in a spasm of wingbeats
then disappeared over a row of tall hemlocks.

For the rest of the day,
I could feel its wild thrumming
against my palms as I wondered about
the hours it must have spent
pent in the shadows of that room,
hidden in the spiky branches
of our decorated tree, breathing there
among the metallic angels, ceramic apples, stars of yarn,
its eyes open, like mine as I lie in bed tonight
picturing this rare, lucky sparrow
tucked into a holly bush now,
a light snow tumbling through the windless dark.

Billy Collins

little tree
little silent Christmas tree
you are so little
you are more like a flower

who found you in the green forest
and were you very sorry to come away?
see   i will comfort you
because you smell so sweetly

i will kiss your cool bark
and hug you safe and tight
just as your mother would,
only don't be afraid

look   the spangles
that sleep all the year in a dark box
dreaming of being taken out and allowed to shine,
the balls the chains red and gold the fluffy threads

put up your little arms
and i'll give them all to you to hold
every finger shall have its ring
and there won't be a single place dark or unhappy

then when you're quite dressed
you'll stand in the window for everyone to see
and how they'll stare !
oh but you'll be very proud

and my little sister and i will take hands
and looking up at our beautiful tree
we'll dance and sing
"Noel Noel"

E. E. Cummings (1894 - 1962)

Mistletoe

Sitting under the mistletoe
(Pale-green, fairy mistletoe),
One last candle burning low,
All the sleepy dancers gone,
Just one candle burning on,
Shadows lurking everywhere:
Some one came, and kissed me there.

Tired I was; my head would go
Nodding under the mistletoe
(Pale-green, fairy mistletoe),
No footsteps came, no voice, but only,
Just as I sat there, sleepy, lonely,
Stooped in the still and shadowy air
Lips unseen - and kissed me there.

Walter de la Mare (1873 - 1956)

Carol

There's a print on the grass
Where she lay, she lay

there's dew on the thorn
where she rapt him away

there's white over green
where she gave him the breast

sancta
sancta simplicitas

O queen of bliss
in the hawthorn shade

O white under white
of the Christchild laid

like a tear, like a tear
in a stem of glass

sancta
sancta simplicitas

Pauline Stainer

A Christmas Song

> Christmas is coming. The goose is getting fat.
> Please put a penny in the old man's hat.
> If you haven't got a penny, a ha'penny will do.
> If you haven't got a ha'penny, God bless you.

Tonight the wide, wet flakes of snow
Drift down like Christmas suicides,
Layering the eaves and boughs until
The landscape seems transformed, as from
A night of talk or love. I've come
From cankered ports and railroad hubs
To winter in a northern state:
Three months of wind and little light.
Wood split, flue cleaned, and ashes hauled,
I am now proof against the cold
And make a place before the stove.
Mired fast in middle age, possessed
Of staved-in barn and brambled lot,
I think of that fierce-minded woman
Whom I loved, painting in a small,
Unheated room, or of a friend,
Sharp-ribbed from poverty, who framed
And fitted out his house by hand
And writes each night by kerosene.
I think, that is, of others who
Withdrew from commerce and the world
To work for joy instead of gain.
O that I could gather them
This Yuletide, and shower them with coins.

Norman Williams

Carol of the Birds

Feet that could be clawed, but are not...
Arms that might have flown, but did not...
No one said, 'Let there be angels!' but the birds

Whose choirs fling alleluias over the sea,
Herring gulls, black backs carolling raucously
While cormorants dry their wings on a rocky stable.

Plovers that stoop to sanctify the land
And scoop small, roundy mangers in the sand,
Swaddle a saviour each in a speckled shell.

A chaffinchy fife unreeling in the marsh
Accompanies the tune a solo thrush
Half sings, half talks in riffs of wordless words,

As hymns flare up from tiny muscled throats,
Robins and hidden wrens whose shiny notes
Tinsel the precincts of the winter sun.

What loftier organ than these pipes of beech,
Pillars resounding with the jackdaws' speech,
And poplars swayed with light like shaken bells?

Wings that could be hands, but are not...
Cries that might be pleas yet cannot
Question or disinvent the stalker's gun,

Be your own hammerbeam angels of the air
Before in the maze of space, you disappear,
Stilled by our dazzling anthrocentric mills.

Anne Stevenson

In California During the Gulf War

Among the blight-killed eucalypts, among
trees and bushes rusted by Christmas frosts,
the yards and hillsides exhausted by five years of drought,

certain airy white blossoms punctually
reappeared, and dense clusters of pale pink, dark pink-
a delicate abundance. They seemed

like guests arriving joyfully on the accustomed
festival day, unaware of the year's events, not perceiving
the sackcloth others were wearing.

To some of us, the dejected landscape consorted well
with our shame and bitterness. Skies ever-blue,
daily sunshine, disgusted us like smile-buttons.

Yet the blossoms, clinging to thin branches
more lightly than birds alert for flight,
lifted the sunken heart

even against its will.
But not
as symbols of hope: they were flimsy
as our resistance to the crimes committed

- again, again - in our name; and yes, they return,
year after year, and yes, they briefly shone with serene joy
over against the dark glare

of evil days. They are, and their presence
is quietness ineffable - and the bombings are, were,
no doubt will be; that quiet, that huge cacophony

simultaneous. No promise was being accorded, the blossoms
were not doves, there was no rainbow. And when it was claimed
the war had ended, it had not ended.

Denise Levertov (1923 - 1997)

December

The year dwindles and glows
to December's red jewel,
my birth month.

The sky blushes,
and lays its cheek
on the sparkling fields.

Then dusk swaddles the cattle,
their silhouettes
simple as faith.

These nights are gifts,
our hands unwrapping the darkness
to see what we have.

The train rushes, ecstatic,
to where you are,
my bright star.

Carol Ann Duffy